Assessment
Emergent Literacy in Kindergarten

Senior Authors

Dr. Roger C. Farr
Chancellor's Professor and Director of
the Center for Innovation in Assessment,
Indiana University, Bloomington

Dr. Dorothy S. Strickland
The State of New Jersey Professor of Reading,
Rutgers University

Orlando   Boston   Dallas   Chicago   San Diego

Visit *The Learning Site!*
www.harcourtschool.com

Copyright © by Harcourt, Inc.

All rights reserved. No part of this publication may be reproduced or transmitted in any form or by any means, electronic or mechanical, including photocopy, recording, or any information storage and retrieval system, without permission in writing from the publisher.

Teachers using COLLECTIONS may photocopy copying masters in complete pages in sufficient quantities for classroom use only and not for resale.

HARCOURT and the Harcourt Logo are trademarks of Harcourt, Inc.

For permission to reprint copyrighted material, grateful acknowledgment is made to the following sources:

Bantam Doubleday Dell Books for Young Readers: My Friend Whale by Simon James. Copyright © 1991 by Simon James.

Greenwillow Books, a division of William Morrow & Company, Inc.: That Bothered Kate by Sally Noll. Copyright © 1991 by Sally Noll.

Simon & Schuster Books for Young Readers, Simon & Schuster Children's Publishing Division: Nellie's Knot by Ken Brown. Copyright © 1993 by Ken Brown.

Printed in the United States of America

ISBN 0-15-313429-1

2 3 4 5 6 7 8 9 10 073 2002 2001 2000

Table of Contents

- iv What Should Kindergarten Assessment Be?
- 1 Using the Kindergarten Assessment Program
- 2 Managing Your Assessment System
- 3–6 Assessing Beginning Readers

7–18 Kid Watching
- 8–9 Kindergarten Assessment as "Kid Watching"
- 10 Assessing Shared Reading and Writing Experiences
- 11–18 Checklists

19–28 Portfolio Assessment
- 20–22 Using Portfolios with Kindergarten Children
- 23 Getting Started
- 24–25 Conducting Portfolio Conferences
- 26 Basic Steps for Evaluating a Portfolio
- 27–28 Evaluation Checklists

29–76 Emergent Literacy Inventories
- 30–36 Using the Inventories
- 37–39 Phonemic Awareness Interview
- 40 Inventory of Concepts About Print
- 41 Inventory of Emergent Reading
- 42–50 Capital/Lowercase Letter Inventory
- 51–62 Matching Beginning Sounds Inventory
- 63–74 Matching Letters and Beginning Sounds Inventory
- 75–76 Answer Keys

77–90 Theme Tests: 1–12
- 78 Using the Theme Tests
- 91 Performance Assessment
- 92 Introduction
- 93 Story: *That Bothered Kate*
    - 111 Response Activities, Model Papers
- 114 Story: *Nellie's Knot*
    - 135 Response Activities, Model Papers
- 138 Story: *My Friend Whale*
    - 149 Response Activities, Model Papers

What Should Kindergarten Assessment Be?

Children's language develops quickly when they are in kindergarten. They are incessant explorers who make sense of their world by talking about it, acting things out, and comparing new things with things they already understand. They write with pictures and scribbles and all sorts of invented spelling. They listen eagerly to new stories and explanations, and they learn to recognize that print represents the stories we read to them.

Getting to Know the Children

Getting to know your children is the primary and continuing challenge of assessment. This means taking a series of closer looks at each child's language development over time—his or her speaking, listening, reading, and writing. A thorough assessment program relies on kid watching, collections of work samples in portfolios, discussions with children about their work samples, and periodic assessments.

Focusing on Language

Since it is impossible to separate all that a child is from his or her language, the focus of assessment is on the whole child, with a special emphasis on language. Oral language, the primary source of a young child's emergent literacy, becomes particularly important when you are assessing kindergartners. Therefore, observations of children in natural settings that encourage interaction should be the main source of information about their growth.

Integrating and Sharing What You Learn

Information for curriculum planning is one outcome of a comprehensive, ongoing assessment program. More than this, knowledge of your children's language development is something you can share with them. Children who recognize and take pride in their emergent literacy are children who are partners with you in their own education.

Using the Kindergarten Assessment Program

To assess children's progress in kindergarten, take a minute to think about your own teaching style and about the assessment goals for kindergartens in your district.

Assessing the Group

One of your main concerns may be to know how the group is doing as a whole, particularly at the beginning of the year. In this case, you will want to refer to the assessment pages at the end of every theme in the *Teacher's Edition*. These oral and written activities will help you informally evaluate how everyone is working together.

Assessing Shared Reading

You may want to collect information about the effectiveness of the shared reading experiences you're providing for your children. If so, use the checklist for shared reading on page 11 of this booklet. You may also find useful the Informal Assessment notes that appear next to the shared reading activities throughout both volumes of the *Teacher's Edition*.

Assessing Each Child

To zero in on individual children's progress, this booklet offers you several methods of assessment, all of which can be integrated into the classroom environment:
- "Kid Watching"
- Portfolio Assessment
- Emergent Literacy Inventories
- Theme Tests
- Performance Assessment

The management grid on the next page shows how to use these methods of assessment throughout the year.

Managing Your Assessment System

What	Where to Find It	When	Child's Task	Teacher's Task
Informal Assessment Notes	*Teacher's Edition*	Ongoing		Watches and listens for specific behaviors as children complete a task.
"Kid Watching"	*Teacher's Edition; Assessment: Emergent Literacy in Kindergarten*	Ongoing	Engages in literacy activities arising naturally in daily school activities.	Observes and records information on anecdotal record sheets or in diaries.
End-of-Theme Assessment	*Teacher's Edition*	Monthly (approx.)	Participates in a guided group activity.	Leads activity; observes groups' responses; may conduct portfolio conferences.
Theme Tests	*Assessment: Emergent Literacy in Kindergarten*	Monthly (approx.)	Completes paper-and-pencil tasks.	Leads child through items; familiarizes child with test format.
Portfolio Assessment	*Assessment: Emergent Literacy in Kindergarten*	3 times a year	Selects and discusses written materials with teacher.	Discusses reading and writing with child; takes notes.
Emergent Literacy Inventories	*Assessment: Emergent Literacy in Kindergarten*	As needed during the year	Varies with type of inventory; see pages 29–41.	Varies with type of inventory; see pages 29–41.
Performance Assessment	*Assessment: Emergent Literacy in Kindergarten*	3 times a year	Listens and responds to an unfamiliar, illustrated story.	Reads story; uses a written activity to assess child's understanding of story elements.

Assessing Beginning Readers

"Good assessment is part of instruction."
–Dr. Roger C. Farr

How to proceed when you must test young children

Formal assessment in kindergarten poses several challenges, one of them being the concern that young children are notoriously unreliable test-takers. Still, useful information can be gleaned from assessment results, and the process itself can reveal a lot about a child. Therefore, anything a teacher can do to help children perform at their best can make a tremendous difference in test scores and can result in more positive attitudes toward school and test-taking.

How can you be sure the test experience doesn't become traumatic for the children?

Think of the assessment as an opportunity to help children become more literate and to assist your teaching. Tests are only a limited sample of a child's achievement, but they can provide useful information about what a child can do. If you approach the assessment as an activity that can produce useful information, your attitude is certain to carry over into student performance.

Above all, treat the assessment session as you would any other class activity. Introduce the assessment to the children as an interesting activity. They may have older brothers and sisters who have discussed *tests* at home, so you may want to avoid that term. Of course, you want the children to give their best efforts on the assessment, but avoid doing anything that will create anxiety.

What should you do if some children can't or won't do the assessments?

First, make sure that children understand what they are to do. Make sure that each child is on-task—at the right place on the correct page. Be certain that children understand the directions. Unless test directions prohibit doing so, prepare children by creating an activity with similar procedures and let them experience it sometime before the assessment is administered.

Have children practice test formats and procedures. Familiarize children with test formats and procedures, while presenting them as just another activity. Some assessments provide a practice test; check to see if one is available, or make up an activity that is similar to the kinds of questions and the ways of responding that the test will require. For example: Will the children be expected to fill in ovals above or below pictures? Will they circle objects or pictures? Have children try these procedures as a regular class activity. If children will not be allowed to talk while taking a test, present an activity beforehand in which they are asked not to talk to each other. When you do get to any sample items on the test itself, take the time to be sure that *each* child has responded to them correctly.

Don't let children who seem unable or unwilling to respond to the assessment sit by idly. Provide children who do not go ahead with the assessment activity with an alternate activity so that they are occupied while their classmates work on the assessments.

What do you do if children want to talk and ask questions during the test?

The directions to many assessments will direct you not to allow this, but if they do not, use common sense and allow what you can within the guidelines. The idea is to help children feel at ease while being tested. Again, including activities similar to the assessment in the class experience before the test is given is a good idea.

What are some other ways you can help children perform as well as they can?

Follow the instructions carefully in administering assessments, but, if allowed, you can follow these recommendations:

1. If you have a choice, administer the assessment in the morning when children are freshest.
2. Break up longer assessments into smaller sessions if possible.
3. Watch for children who may come to school in the morning upset or hungry. If you can delay the assessment for such children, do so. If you can give them a snack or alleviate their distress, do that.
4. You may have an idea which children are likely to have trouble with the testing procedures. You can situate them so that you can get to them easily to provide assistance.
5. If possible, arrange to have an aide or assistant familiar to the children in the classroom on the day of the assessment. The aide may help administer the assessment and attend to individual children.

Should you find out what is on the tests and drill your children on them?

The tests you will be asked to administer have almost certainly been developed and selected on the basis of goals that guide your instruction. If you have taught well, and if the children understand the format and testing procedures, they will probably perform well. Don't drill on specific content. It is not appropriate, and it has been argued that it hinders, not helps, student performance.

Should you send a note home to parents about the upcoming assessment?

This may depend on your school or the district. Sometimes notices of assessments are sent automatically to all parents. Sometimes newspapers carry information about the testing. If the choice is up to you, it would be best to send a note telling the parents that a test will be given. However, you should emphasize that it is not a test that the parents or children should be concerned about. Report any rationale the state or system has presented for the assessment, and explain that the assessment is just like the things their children have been doing in class. Caution them not to make a "big deal" of the assessment with their children. They should, however, be sure that the children have rested as well as possible the night before and have had a good breakfast the morning of the day the assessment is to be given.

How should you present the results of the assessment to parents if asked to do so?

Prepare for the report by understanding and thinking about the results. Be certain that you understand the reported results of the assessment before talking to parents about them. Read the interpretation manual carefully. After you understand the results, set them in a context of the other activities the child has been doing in class. Has the child performed about the same as he or she has on the other activities? Better? Worse? Prepare a bit by thinking about why you think this may be so. Show parents other work by the child that demonstrates other degrees of strong or weak performance.

Above all, emphasize that the assessment is only one kind of information. Whether or not a child has performed well or poorly on a test, be sure to explain to parents that the assessment is but one activity. It produces only one kind of information about what kind of language user and thinker the child is. Consider evidence you have from a child's other activities and your observations that underline or endorse the test results. Be ready with some suggestions of ways the parents can help their children.

How can I make the best use of the assessment results?

Examine the results critically. Review the results to see what valid information they may give about the instruction of both individual children and the whole class. In particular, you should compare the results to other evidence you have collected on student performance on other activities and through observation. Do these test results confirm what you already know about a student, or do they surprise you? How can any discrepancies between these results and your own knowledge of a child be resolved? What instructional emphases and approaches might the results recommend?

Let the assessment reveal how your students handle tasks like those that make up the test activities. The very best information you can get from an assessment can be gathered while the assessment is in progress. Watch the children carefully as they work on the tests. What do they do with each task? What seems to give the group or individuals problems? What kinds of questions do they have? How persistent are they? What kind of work habits are revealed? What else does this interesting classroom activity reveal to you?

Guidelines for Assessing Beginning Readers

Most importantly, good assessment is *part of instruction*. The observations you make, the notes you take, and the discussions you have are all vital aspects of assessment. These guidelines should help to assure that assessment time is useful and productive in helping you to plan instruction.

1. Always see that the assessment reveals what each child *can* do. Give every child an opportunity to be successful.
2. Make sure that assessment is not intimidating. Make it a normal part of classroom activities.
3. Let children behave and respond as naturally as the test instructions allow.
4. Be sure the children understand what is expected of them. Present testing procedures and formats ahead of time as a practice, if possible.
5. Be certain that parents understand the purpose of the assessment, what the results mean, and that the results are but one piece of information about the performance of their children.
6. Look on assessment as an opportunity to observe children, to learn some things about their use of language, and to verify and strengthen your instructional goals.
7. Maintain the perspective that assessment has instructional value.

Kid Watching

Kid Watching

Assessing Shared Reading and Writing Experiences

Checklists

"Putting the 'kid watching' philosophy to work in the kindergarten classroom involves observation, interaction, and analysis."

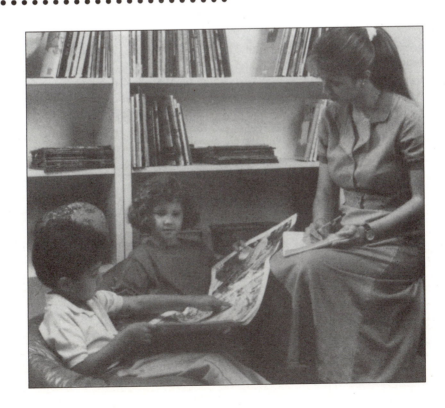

Kindergarten Assessment as "Kid Watching"

Kindergarten teachers are continually monitoring children's development. They start by establishing the emotional as well as the physical environment for learning. Within this context, they offer children many kinds of experiences. Some involve teacher-guided group instruction, such as shared reading and response to literature. Other experiences are geared more to cooperative learning and personal choice, such as center-based activities. Still other activities involve teacher and child in one-on-one instruction.

A good kindergarten program offers a balance between teacher-guided and child-centered experiences. Effective teachers know that by "kid watching" as children participate in these activities, they can build a viable profile of each child as a learner. Kid watching, the process of monitoring children's ongoing development through daily activities that are integral to instruction, is at the center of such an assessment program.

Putting the kid-watching philosophy to work in the kindergarten classroom involves observation, interaction, and analysis (Goodman, 1989, p. 8).

Observation

Observation includes the examination of what children are doing as the teacher stands on the sidelines. Very often, the teacher focuses on an individual child working independently or as a member of a group. (See the record-keeping forms on pages 12–18 of this booklet.)

Sometimes, however, the teacher may also want to watch a small group of children in action during center time. Are they making use of print in the environment? Do they seem to be applying strategies introduced during teacher-guided instruction? Are the

materials in the center serving their purpose? How might the center function more effectively?

One way to streamline your note taking when observing is to jot down impressions on self-stick notes. Later, put them in a child's folder or portfolio, or in your own records about center activity.

Interaction

Interaction enables a teacher to gather information during conferences about work in progress. A teacher's questions help both teacher and child discover what the child knows. (See pages 24–25.) Teacher-child dialogues about a story or a drawing, the "reading" of a favorite book, or the literacy events that occur during free-play activities yield excellent information about how well a child is using his or her emergent literacy.

Most often, these interactions will be brief encounters that take advantage of opportune or "teachable" moments. For that reason, it helps to keep note cards or other materials handy at all times for record keeping.

Analysis

Analysis of literacy activities—reading stories, writing responses to a big book, inventing conversations between two homemade puppets—is an in-depth study of children's language awareness and language use. A teacher uses his or her psycholinguistic and sociolinguistic knowledge to understand where children are and what can be done to help them progress as emerging readers and writers.

Information from the three processes described above helps confirm what a teacher may already know intuitively about his or her children. Pages 10–11 describe how these kid-watching tools may be used during a shared reading or shared writing.

Reference

Goodman, Yetta. "Evaluation of Students." In K.S. Goodman, Y. M. Goodman, and W. Hood (Eds.).

The Whole Language Evaluation Book. Heinemann: 1989.

Assessing Shared Reading and Writing Experiences

Shared reading and writing naturally include a great deal of child/teacher interaction. What we know about first-language learning and parent/child interaction during family storybook reading tells us that shared reading helps children learn to read almost as effortlessly as they learned to talk. Similarly, during shared writing experiences children observe various writing behaviors modeled. The chart below shows how this works.

Roles of Teacher and Child During Shared Reading and Writing	
Teacher	**Child**
Presents whole tasks	Experiences whole tasks
Gives active support	Gains knowledge; enjoys reading
Intervenes when needed	Internalizes textual frameworks and language patterns
Gradually releases support	Internalizes strategies
Offers opportunities for child to apply new learning	Practices strategies using whole texts in meaningful ways

Assessment During Shared Reading and Writing

The checklists on the facing page can be used in two ways. First, they can help you monitor the overall progress of the group or the progress of specific individuals whose needs are especially challenging. Second, the checklists are reminders of the major purposes for shared reading and writing. All teachers have their favorite stories and writing forms, each one especially good for teaching a few specific skills and strategies. A checklist helps ensure that none of these concepts are missed.

Observing and Analyzing

Most children really enjoy whole-group literacy experiences. When you have a child who doesn't seem to, naturally you want to know why. Is this due to a problem with learning the language? Could it be a visual or auditory problem that should be checked by a professional? Is the child shy? Or, perhaps you have a child who is functioning at a very advanced level. You may want to observe this child more closely, to determine whether he or she is ready for more challenging materials. The checklist will help you know what to look for in these individuals.

Checklist for Monitoring Shared Reading

Children demonstrate understanding of the following concepts:

- ☐ Print contains meaning
- ☐ Pictures convey and enhance meaning
- ☐ Left-to-right direction
- ☐ Book title, author, etc.
- ☐ Words, letters, etc.
- ☐ Discuss meanings related to characters and events
- ☐ Make and confirm reasonable predictions
- ☐ Infer words in cloze activities
- ☐ Remember sequence of events

Checklist for Monitoring Shared Writing

Children demonstrate the following behaviors:

- ☐ Show interest in writing
- ☐ Understand that writing has a variety of functions
- ☐ Participate in stages of the writing process
- ☐ Contribute ideas about a topic
- ☐ Voluntarily use classroom writing center
- ☐ Refer to class-composed stories, letters, charts
- ☐ View themselves as writers

Listening

....

Child's Name: _____

    1 = no behavior   2 = beginning behavior

    3 = developing behavior   4 = secure behavior

	Date	Date	Date
Distinguishes individual sounds in a word (phonemic awareness)			
Responds to simple directions, commands, and questions			
Acquires new vocabulary words			
Listens and responds to oral readings			
Listens to peers			
Focuses attention on a speaker			
Responds meaningfully in conversation			
Hears and responds to repetitive speech sounds			
Appreciates prose, poetry, and rhymes			
Listens for information			
Follows three-step oral directions			

Comments:
_____
_____
_____
_____

12   Assessment: Emergent Literacy in Kindergarten

Speaking

Child's Name: _____

1 = no behavior   2 = beginning behavior
3 = developing behavior   4 = secure behavior

	Date	Date	Date
Uses language to satisfy personal needs (hygiene, self-help, etc.)			
Initiates conversations with teacher and with peers			
Describes objects and pictures			
Role-plays in a variety of situations (alone or with others)			
Retells stories and repeats songs			
Is aware of appropriate speaking behavior and voice volume			
Relates ideas in a logical order			
Shares facts and information			
Asks relevant questions in a variety of situations			
Reads aloud			

Comments:

_____

_____

_____

Kid Watching 13

Reading

Child's Name: _____

1 = no behavior 2 = beginning behavior
3 = developing behavior 4 = secure behavior

	Date	Date	Date
Recognizes environmental print			
Recognizes own name in print			
Enjoys listening to stories			
Participates in shared reading activities			
Voluntarily looks at books			
Handles a book correctly (holds right side up, turns pages, etc.)			
Recalls details from familiar stories			
Retells stories in a logical order			
Uses pictures to gain meaning from text			
Responds to stories through interpretive activities (art, drama, etc.)			
Recognizes that print contains meaning			
Recognizes common or important words in stories			
Retells own stories			

Comments:

_____

_____

_____

_____

Auditory and Visual Awareness

Child's Name: _____

1 = no behavior 2 = beginning behavior
3 = developing behavior 4 = secure behavior

	Date	Date	Date
Identifies rhyming words			
Recognizes letter names			
Matches capital and lowercase letters			
Matches repeated words in stories			
Identifies word boundaries			
Discriminates between beginning sounds			
Matches beginning sounds			
Practices phonemic segmentation			
Associates beginning sounds with corresponding consonants			
Recognizes word family patterns			

Comments:

_____
_____
_____

Writing

Child's Name: _____

1 = no behavior 2 = beginning behavior
3 = developing behavior 4 = secure behavior

	Date	Date	Date
Voluntarily writes			
Participates in shared writing—narrative, functional, informational			
Draws pictures and tells stories about them			
Writes own name			
Dictates captions or stories about pictures			
Uses personal experiences as source of ideas for writing			
Enjoys sharing compositions with peers			
Records information			
Asks how to spell words			

Comments:

_____

_____

_____

Writing Conventions

Child's Name: _____

    1 = no behavior   2 = beginning behavior

    3 = developing behavior   4 = secure behavior

	Date	Date	Date
Prints letters legibly with correct pencil grip and beginning stroke			
Prints symbols horizontally, from left to right			
Uses mostly scribble writing			
Uses mostly letter strings or random letters			
Often uses a single letter to represent a whole word			
Uses temporary spelling to write words			
Leaves spaces between words			
Uses some vowels in spelling			
Makes transition between temporary spelling and conventional spelling			
Shows awareness of how to use capital and lowercase forms			
Begins to use punctuation			

Comments:
_____
_____
_____
_____

Thinking

Child's Name: _____

1 = no behavior 2 = beginning behavior
3 = developing behavior 4 = secure behavior

	Date	Date	Date
Uses all senses to observe environment			
Builds on prior knowledge			
Sequences events and stories			
Recognizes cause and effect			
Classifies / categorizes			
Distinguishes between real and make-believe			
Predicts outcomes			
Draws reasonable conclusions			
Interprets viewpoints and feelings			

Comments:
_____
_____
_____
_____

Portfolio Assessment

Using Portfolios

Getting Started

Conducting Portfolio Conferences

Basic Steps for Evaluating a Portfolio

Evaluation Checklists

"Evaluation is not something that is done *to* children, but rather *for* and *by* children."

Using Portfolios with Kindergarten Children

Portfolio assessment is child-centered, contributing to an environment where learning flourishes. Using portfolios, children share collections of their work and interact with others to discuss it. As an outcome, children gain confidence in themselves and in their abilities.

What Are Portfolios?

Portfolios can be many different things and can be used in many different ways. Physically, a portfolio can be a folder, a box, or space on a shelf. The one physical element that portfolios have in common is that they are places or containers in which children's work is collected. Portfolios can include work samples in the form of finished products, first drafts, notes, lists, and pictures.

A portfolio system is based on the belief that portfolios should help children take ownership of their own literacy development. Portfolios can also provide teachers with a more comprehensive basis on which to judge children's progress than can traditional tests. Integrated reading and writing portfolios

- are an integral part of the total reading / writing program.
- provide many opportunities for children to show what they can do and what they are proud of.
- provide a focus for child-teacher and child-child discussions about reading and writing ideas and interests.
- give children a sense of control over their own literacy development.
- serve as a springboard to more reading and writing activities.
- include finished and unfinished work, pictures, and lists of writing ideas.
- are an effective instructional tool and not merely another way to evaluate children's reading and writing.

Why Should Portfolios Be Used?

Using portfolios is not a new idea. Indeed, teachers have always collected samples of children's work, discussed with children their favorite books and stories, and talked with them about their writing.

For children, the portfolio system

- enhances self-esteem because portfolios emphasize what they *can* do.
- provides an opportunity for them to be responsible for their own learning as they reflect on their reading and writing.
- is noncompetitive because each child's portfolio reflects his or her unique development.

For teachers, the portfolio system
- ◆ provides regular opportunities to talk with children about their literacy development and about their reading and writing interests and attitudes.
- ◆ provides a method of continual informal assessment for the purpose of instructional planning.

What Does a Portfolio System Look Like?

For children, part of the fun of portfolios is making their own. Here are some classroom-tested ideas you can choose from:

Each child decorates his or her own folder.

Each child uses a shopping bag to store materials.

Each child decorates his or her own shoe box.

Each child has his or her own space on a shelf.

Portfolio Assessment

Children's portfolios should be readily accessible to them so that they can add materials, work on unfinished pictures and stories, and share with other children what they've done. You will begin to realize that these portfolios are not merely storage places for keeping children's finished or best work, but are working portfolios that help children take responsibility for their ongoing progress.

Regularly scheduled teacher-child conferences are an important component of a portfolio system. Since kindergartners' abilities and interests vary widely, a conference with one child may consist of talking about pictures he or she has drawn, while another child may want to read a book he or she has written and illustrated. Frequent impromptu conferences to discuss particular works in progress are also part of a portfolio system.

A teacher reviews children's portfolios to plan instruction, to write reports to family members, to prepare for parent-teacher conferences, and to evaluate the progress being made by individual children and by the group as a whole.

How Can a Portfolio System Be Managed?

Keeping track of all the reading and writing children do, helping children collect work to keep in their portfolios, and reviewing the contents of portfolios might, at first, seem like an impossible management task for teachers. However, it needn't be difficult at all. If you use portfolios as part of your ongoing reading/language arts program, you will find that they actually lessen your work and help you better organize your instruction. The most important factor in using portfolios is to remember that the portfolios belong to the children—ownership of and pride in their work is key.

Getting Started

Follow these suggestions to start a successful portfolio system:

- **Portfolios should be a normal part of your classroom routine.**
Talk with children about the use of the portfolios. Emphasize that their portfolios are special places in which to keep their reading and writing work.

- **Children need to feel a sense of ownership of their portfolios.**
Encourage children to write their names on their portfolios. They may want to paste or draw favorite story characters on the covers.

- **Portfolios should be easily accessible to children.**
Portfolios should be kept in a place in the classroom where children can find them easily and use them daily.

- **Be sure that children understand that the portfolios are their responsibility.**
One of the most important features of any portfolio system is that children become actively involved in their own literacy development. You can further encourage children in portfolio conferences by asking them about other books they have read and other writing they have done.

- **Don't make the portfolios a testing program.**
Portfolio conferences are a time for you and your child to discuss his or her reading and writing ideas, interests, and development. Don't use them as a time to grade children.

- **During portfolio conferences, you will learn a great deal about children and their developing reading and writing interests and abilities.**
The portfolio conference should be a time for a child to show off his or her favorite piece of writing, to discuss a favorite book or story, or to talk about things that he or she would like to read and write about. Through these discussions, you will learn far more about the child than you could ever learn from a formal test.

"Portfolios should be a normal part of your classroom routine."

Conducting Portfolio Conferences

Conferences should be a regular part of your reading/language arts program.

What Are the Essentials of a Conference?

Conferences are really quite simple. All you have to do is remember that a conference is a time for sharing and that you are having a conversation with a person who has much to offer. Here are some guidelines:

1. **Allow the child to do most of the talking.** You will learn much more about the child if you let him or her talk.

2. **Avoid being evaluative.** Respect the child as a learner. If you think of the conference as a time for the child to reflect on his or her own reading and writing, you will be less likely to be judgmental.

3. **Avoid interruptions.** Children need our undivided attention during a conference. If you are constantly interrupted, the child will be unable to develop his or her ideas.

4. **Ask questions that open up conversations rather than shut down communication.** Use open-ended questions that ask for explanations, expansions, examples, and discussion. You learn more about children when they explain, justify, clarify, and express their ideas and beliefs.

5. **Use the conference as a time to plan goals with the child.** Ask questions like *What do you plan to read or write about next? What are you planning to do with this story? How can I help you?*

6. **Write notes about what you have learned.** Take time after each conference to jot down notes about the conference and the goals you and the child have discussed. Add the notes to the child's portfolio so that they can be reviewed at the next conference.

Child's Name _____ Date _____

Conference Checklist

- ☐ is willing to share ideas
- ☐ shows confidence and risk-taking in experimenting with new ideas
- ☐ uses information from other models, for example, from other authors and genres or from friends
- ☐ explores personal interests through reading and writing
- ☐ is aware of audience
- ☐ gives evidence of how feedback from others has been incorporated into reading and writing
- ☐ uses expressive language in discussing a previously read book or a selected piece of writing

General Question/Statement	Follow-Up Questions
1. Tell me how you use your portfolio.	Why did you organize your portfolio this way? How did you decide which pieces to include in your portfolio?
2. Tell me about one story in your portfolio.	Why is this story important to you? Why did you choose to write this? Where did you get the idea? Would you like to read it to me? Did you have any problems writing it?
3. Tell me about a book that you have read.	Explain to me why this book is important to you. Why did you decide to read this book? Why would someone else like reading it?
4. What are you going to read and write next?	How can I help you with this? What will you do first? Is there someone with whom you would like to work?

Portfolio Assessment

BASIC STEPS FOR EVALUATING A PORTFOLIO

STEP 1
Review the child's reading and writing.

An evaluation of the amount and quality of reading and writing is a subjective judgment. For example, what is outstanding for one child may be average for another. Your goal should be to evaluate each child's progress over time. Remember to review the notes that you make during your portfolio conferences.

STEP 2
Review the child's interests and attitudes.

Some children include a wide variety of reading and writing materials in their portfolios, while others include only a limited range. One of your goals will be to help the child broaden his or her literacy activities.

It is important to use the portfolio as a primary source of evidence of the child's attitudes and interests. If you base your evaluation only on other classroom behaviors, you may misjudge a child who is in fact an eager reader and writer but who doesn't outwardly show enthusiasm during class.

STEP 3
Review the child's use of reading/writing strategies.

The most important goal in teaching reading and writing is to help children develop effective strategies. As you review the child's use of reading/writing strategies, make sure that you carefully examine

- the child's work produced during theme projects and in various centers.

- the child's comments about his or her own reading and writing. The child's reflections can help you determine how he or she is progressing as a reader and writer and which strategies are and are not being used.

- the child's reactions to what has been read. A child's comments often give insight into his or her developing interests and reading strategies. For example, you can note whether a child relates what has been read to personal experiences.

Review of Portfolio Reading Materials

Child's Name: _____

Teacher's Name: _____

Date: _____ Grade: _____ School: _____

1 = Limited   2 = Below expectation   3 = Average   4 = Above expectation   5 = Outstanding

Assessment	1	2	3	4	5	Teacher Comments
Emergent reading skills						
Recognizes speech/print relationship						
Understands concepts of letters/words						
Handles books appropriately						
Attitudes toward reading						
Chooses reading during free time						
Reads many books/stories						
Listens attentively to stories						
Reading interests						
Has favorite books/stories						
Retells familiar stories						
Participates in discussions about books/stories						
Reading skills/strategies						
Constructs meaning when reading						
Relates stories to background						
Shows confidence as a reader						

Summary Assessment

Assessment	For This Review			Since Last Review		
	Outstanding	Average	Limited	Improving	About the Same	Seems Poorer
Amount of reading						
Attitudes toward reading						
Reading skills/strategies						

Review of Portfolio Writing Materials

Child's Name: _____

Teacher's Name: _____

Date: _____ Grade: _____ School: _____

1 = Limited   2 = Below expectation   3 = Average   4 = Above expectation   5 = Outstanding

Assessment	1	2	3	4	5	Teacher Comments
Emergent writing skills						
Draws to convey meaning						
Writes his or her name						
Writes capital letters						
Writes lowercase letters						
Attitudes toward writing						
Shows enthusiasm for writing						
Combines drawing and writing						
Writing Skills						
Participates in prewriting activities						
Writes for specific audiences						
Focuses on meaning						
Mechanics						
Demonstrates increasing control of penmanship						
Uses spacing between words						
Writes left to right						

Summary Assessment

Assessment	For This Review			Since Last Review		
	Outstanding	Average	Limited	Improving	About the Same	Seems Poorer
Amount of writing and drawing						
Attitudes toward writing and drawing						
Quality of writing						

Emergent Literacy Inventories

Using the Inventories

Phonemic Awareness Interview

Inventory of Concepts About Print and Emergent Reading

Capital/Lowercase Letter Inventory

Matching Beginning Sounds Inventory

Matching Letters and Beginning Sounds Inventory

Answer Key

"Systematic, regular assessment for each child is the goal."

Using the Inventories

The Phonemic Awareness Interview (pages 37–39)

Phonemic awareness is an understanding that speech is composed of a series of individual sounds (phonemes). A child who demonstrates an ability to orally manipulate phonemes is likely to be successful in reading. Children who have difficulty attending to and manipulating the sounds in their language are likely to have problems learning to read. These children need additional experience with oral language play to heighten their sensitivity to the phonemic basis of speech.

The Phonemic Awareness Interview is an oral test designed to provide information about a child's level of phonemic awareness to help the teacher plan literacy activities. The Interview consists of four tasks, each one measuring a different aspect of phonemic awareness: 1) sound matching, 2) sound isolation, 3) sound blending, and 4) sound segmenting. The tasks are sequenced from the easiest to the most difficult. You may use any one, or all, of the tasks to assess each child. A model, a sample item, and test items are provided for each task. As the child responds orally to each item, record the child's responses on the recording form.

General Testing Considerations

Administer the Interview individually in a quiet and comfortable setting. This will help ensure that the child attends to the task and can give the teacher insights into problems the child may be having.

There is no time limit; however, a period of 15–20 minutes is suggested. It is recommended that all tasks be administered in a single session, but they can be given separately over several days if necessary.

Become familiar with the directions and test items. The text in bold type is intended to be read aloud. The other information is for the teacher only and should not be read aloud. However, you should feel free to rephrase the directions, to repeat the sample, or to give additional examples to make sure the child understands what to do.

You and the child should be seated at a flat table or desk. The best seating location for you is facing the child, to facilitate clear diction and immediate recording. Before beginning an Interview, spend a few minutes in light, friendly conversation with the child. Don't refer to the Interview as a "test." Tell the child you would like to play some "word games."

Specific Testing Considerations

Follow these steps for a Phonemic Awareness Interview:

1. Duplicate a copy of the "Phonemic Awareness Interview Administering/Recording Form" for each task and one "Summary of Performance Form" for each child. You will record a child's responses on the "Administering/Recording Form" and the totals on the "Summary of Performance Form." The child will not need any materials.

2. Explain that the words the child hears and says every day are made up of sounds and that you will be saying some words and sounds and asking questions about them. It will be helpful to the child if you accentuate each word, syllable, or phoneme by prolonging and pausing between words and sounds.

3. Begin the Interview with Task 1, Sound Matching, and proceed through Task 4, Sound Segmenting. If the child has difficulty with the first few items or cannot answer them, you may wish to discontinue conducting the Interview until a later time. If the child misses half of the items at any task, move on to the next task.

4. After the Interview, record the child's scores on the "Summary of Performance Form." Use the scale in the box to determine the level that best describes the child's understanding of phonemic awareness. Children whose scores reflect minimal or limited understanding may need additional oral language experiences.

The Inventory of Concepts About Print and Emergent Reading (pages 40–41)

Suggestions for Administering

Each child should be assessed individually about three times during the kindergarten year. September/October, December/January, and April/May are suggested times. Since this is an individual assessment, it is not necessary for all children to be assessed during the same week or specific time period. Systematic, regular assessment for each child is the goal.

Using the Results

Use the checklists, along with other anecdotal records and portfolio samples, to assemble a reading/writing profile of each child. At parent/teacher conferences, use all the information you have compiled to

◆ emphasize what the child can do.

◆ explain your short- and long-term goals for the child.

◆ help family members understand your reading/language arts program.

◆ make suggestions for things family members can do at home with the child.

References

Clay, M. The Early Detection of Reading Difficulties. Portsmouth, NH: Heinemann Educational, 1979.

Sulzby, E. "Children's Emergent Reading of Favorite Storybooks: A Developmental Study." Reading Research Quarterly, 20, 451–458, 1985.

Capital/Lowercase Letter Inventory (pages 42–50)

General Testing Considerations

You may wish to use this inventory at the beginning of the year to assess children's general awareness of letter forms. The results will help you plan curriculum and match activities with children's level of familiarity with letters.

Conduct another inventory toward the end of the year to assess how well each child can match capital and lowercase letters. Children having difficulty recognizing specific letters may need additional practice with those letters. See the Phonics Workshops throughout the *Teacher's Edition*, as well as phonics lessons for specific letters.

Specific Testing Considerations

Tell children to find the sample box with the star at the top of page 42. Say: **Look at the first letter in the box. It is a capital *F*. Does everyone see the capital *F*?** Pause; allow time for children to find the letter. Then say: **Now look at the other three letters in that row. Find the lowercase *f*.** Pause; allow time for children to look at each letter. Call on a child to supply the correct answer. Then say: **Yes, the last letter is a lowercase *f*. The lowercase *f* matches the capital *F*. So fill in the last answer circle under the lowercase *f*.**

Check to be sure children have filled in the correct answer circle, and help anyone who has difficulty. Then say: **Now put your pencils on the number 1. Look at the first letter in that row. Find the letter that is the capital form of the letter. Fill in the answer circle under it.**

Pause while children mark their answers. Say: **Does everyone understand what to do? You will see a letter at the beginning of each row. If it is a capital letter, you will find the matching lowercase letter. If the first letter in the row is a lowercase letter, you will find the matching capital letter. When you find the matching letter, fill in the answer circle under the letter, and go on to the next row. Keep working until you come to the word *Stop!* When you come to the word *Stop!*, put your pencils down and sit quietly until everyone has finished.**

Matching Beginning Sounds Inventory (pages 51–62)

General Testing Considerations

You may wish to use Part A of this inventory after the middle of the year as a practice test to help children become familiar and comfortable with standardized testing procedures. Part A includes all consonants and vowels taught in Volume 1 of the *Teacher's Edition*.

Use Part B toward the end of the year to assess children's ability to match beginning sounds. Part B includes all consonants except *Q* and *X* and all vowels. Children having difficulty hearing and matching specific initial sounds may benefit from activities in the Phonics Workshops throughout the *Teacher's Edition*, as well as from the phonics lessons for specific letters.

Part A

Tell children to find the box with the hat at the top of the page. Say: **You see a picture of a hat. Listen to the word *hat*. Find the picture that begins with the same sound that you hear at the beginning of the word *hat*. You see pictures of a desk, a house, and a tent.** Pause; allow time for children to look at each picture. Call on a child to supply the correct answer. Then say: **Yes, the word *house* begins with the same sound that you hear at the beginning of the word *hat*. So fill in the answer circle under the house.**

Make sure that children have filled in the correct answer circle, and help anyone who has difficulty. Then say: **Now put your pencils on the picture of the book (row 1). Listen to the word *book*. Find the picture that begins with the same sound that you hear at the beginning of *book*. You see pictures of a mouse, a pig, and a bell. Fill in the answer circle under the picture that begins with the same sound as *book*.**

Pause while children mark their answers. Continue the test following the same procedure.

Stimulus Word	Picture Names
2. milk	feather, cat, moon
3. car	cup, dog, tent
4. puppet	duck, wagon, pie
5. fence	bee, fox, cat
6. sun	van, sock, door
7. alligator	apple, rake, umbrella
8. boy	yarn, jet, book
9. tiger	toothbrush, house, leaf
10. mitten	horn, mouse, jar
11. pig	pencil, fan, cow
12. ax	hat, girl, astronaut
13. sandwich	ball, seal, fish
14. hammer	top, helicopter, king
15. tent	tiger, duck, pencil
16. cat	window, car, yo-yo
17. deer	robot, dog, fish
18. sock	nest, yarn, sun
19. mouse	horse, bear, mop
20. elephant	hat, elf, fence

Part B

Tell children to find the box with the tiger at the top of the page. Say: **You see a picture of a tiger. Listen to the word *tiger*. Find the picture that begins with the same sound that you hear at the beginning of the word *tiger*. You see pictures of a dog, a wagon, and a top.** Pause; allow time for children to look at each picture. Call on a child to supply the correct answer. Then say: **Yes, the word *top* begins with the same sound that you hear at the beginning of the word *tiger*. So fill in the answer circle under the top.**

Make sure that children have filled in the correct answer circle, and help anyone who has difficulty. Then say: **Now put your pencils on the picture of the nine (row 21). Listen to the word *nine*. Find the picture that begins with the same sound that you hear at the beginning of *nine*. You see pictures of a necklace, a book, and a goat. Fill in the answer circle under the picture that begins with the same sound as *nine*.**

Stimulus Word	Picture Names
21. nine	necklace, book, goat
22. pen	desk, pan, moon
23. nut	nail, tiger, bus
24. envelope	elephant, cat, dog
25. sun	tent, soap, book
26. turtle	duck, horse, table
27. vegetables	shoe, vest, king
28. web	house, umbrella, watch
29. rope	rake, hat, top
30. ostrich	king, olive, sandwich
31. leaf	zipper, cage, lion
32. inchworm	table, violin, igloo
33. yarn	leaf, guitar, yo-yo
34. zipper	car, zebra, hat
35. bee	vest, pig, ball
36. car	cage, pencil, hammer
37. dog	house, deer, apple
38. fan	desk, fork, bear
39. olive	girl, book, octopus
40. horse	kitten, heart, violin
41. jacks	igloo, jet, cup
42. kangaroo	keys, soap, tent
43. lion	lock, envelope, saw
44. milk	ax, moon, book
45. octopus	ostrich, vest, yarn
46. watch	horse, web, nail
47. umbrella	jet, fan, up
48. necklace	pen, apple, nail

34 Assessment: Emergent Literacy in Kindergarten

Matching Letters and Beginning Sounds Inventory (pages 63–74)

General Testing Considerations

You may wish to use Part A of this inventory after the middle of the year as a practice test to help children become familiar and comfortable with standardized testing procedures. Part A includes all consonants and vowels taught in Volume 1 of the *Teacher's Edition*.

Use Part B toward the end of the year to assess children's ability to match beginning sounds. Part B includes all consonants except Q and X and all vowels. Children having difficulty hearing and matching specific initial sounds may benefit from activities in the Phonics Workshops throughout the *Teacher's Edition*, as well as from the phonics lessons for specific letters.

Part A

Tell children to find the box with the letter *p* at the top of the page. Say: **You see the letter *p*. Find the picture that begins with the /p/ sound. You see pictures of a bike, a pig, and a tree.** Pause; allow time for children to look at each picture. Call on a child to supply the correct answer. Then say: **Yes, the word *pig* begins with the /p/ sound. So fill in the answer circle under the pig.**

Make sure that children have filled in the correct answer circle, and help anyone who has difficulty. Then say: **Now put your pencils on the letter *m* (row 1). Find the picture that begins with the /m/ sound. You see pictures of a pie, a sun, and a mitten. Fill in the answer circle under the picture that begins with the /m/ sound.**

Pause while children mark their answers. Continue the test following the same procedure.

Stimulus Letter	Picture Names
2. s	seal, fish, bee
3. j	jar, pencil, hat
4. t	bird, car, tent
5. c	sock, cup, basketball
6. f	fence, cat, horse
7. d	mouse, balloon, dog
8. a	sandwich, alligator, bell
9. h	jar, box, hose
10. b	pencil, bib, duck
11. m	bird, fish, mouse
12. c	car, sun, puppet
13. t	wagon, toothbrush, house
14. f	mouse, helicopter, fox
15. p	hammer, pickle, seal
16. d	duck, can, yo-yo
17. s	tent, hose, sock
18. e	fox, envelope, car
19. j	king, jacks, rake
20. h	hammer, sun, mitten
21. t	wagon, toothbrush, house
22. a	bird, pencil, ax
23. s	seal, dog, mop
24. e	elf, cup, tent

Part B

Tell children to find the box with the letter *w* at the top of the page. Say: **You see the letter *w*. Find the picture that begins with the /w/ sound. You see pictures of a leaf, a wagon, and a dog.** Pause; allow time for children to look at each picture. Call on a child to supply the correct answer. Then say: **Yes, the word *wagon* begins with the /w/ sound. So fill in the answer circle under the wagon.**

Make sure that children have filled in the correct answer circle, and help anyone who has difficulty. Then say: **Now put your pencils on the letter *r* (row 25). Find the picture that begins with the /r/ sound. You see pictures of jacks, a vest, and a ring. Fill in the answer circle under the picture that begins with the /r/ sound.**

	Stimulus Letter	Picture Names
26.	o	helicopter, pickle, ostrich
27.	k	nest, king, toothbrush
28.	l	leaf, bell, fish
29.	i	ring, igloo, goat
30.	c	can, rake, pencil
31.	w	seal, bee, wagon
32.	t	hat, zebra, table
33.	v	fence, vest, seal
34.	p	puppet, yo-yo, balloon
35.	n	house, nest, duck
36.	u	tree, car, umbrella
37.	y	dog, bib, yo-yo
38.	f	fish, bike, sock
39.	a	pie, ax, hammer
40.	d	fence, mitten, doll
41.	z	fox, zebra, pig
42.	h	yo-yo, wagon, house
43.	r	mouse, rake, leaf
44.	j	pickle, king, jar
45.	e	tent, elephant, moon
46.	s	king, car, sandwich
47.	g	hammer, goat, pie
48.	u	duck, up, feather

Phonemic Awareness Interview Administering/Recording Form

Task 1: Sound Matching

Task: The child will listen to two words and will indicate if the two words do or do not begin with the same sound.

Model: I am going to say two words. Listen carefully so you can tell me if the two words begin with the same sound. *Monkey, mother.* Listen again: *monkey, mother.* The words begin with the same sound. *Monkey* and *mother* begin with the same sound.

Sample: Listen to these two words: *rain, snow.*

Listen again: *rain, snow.*

Child's name _____

Date _____

Circle child's response.
(Correct response is in bold type.)

leg, lunch	**Same**	Different
duck, pan	Same	**Different**
sun, moon	Same	**Different**
fork, fish	**Same**	Different
chocolate, checkers	**Same**	Different
phone, poem	Same	**Different**
ball, banana	**Same**	Different
red, nut	Same	**Different**

_____/4 _____/4

Score _____/8

Task 2: Sound Isolation

Task: The child will listen to a word and then will produce the initial phoneme in the word.

Model: I am going to say a word. Then I am going to say just the beginning sound. Listen carefully for the beginning sound: *pig*. The beginning sound is /p/.

Sample: Listen to another word. This time you tell me the beginning sound. Listen carefully: *goat*. What is the beginning sound in *goat*? (/g/) You're correct. /g/ is the beginning sound in *goat*. (Note: If the child tells you a letter name, remind the child to tell you the sound.)

Now listen to some more words. Tell me the beginning sound you hear in each word.

Child's name _____

Date _____

	Correct Response	Child's Response
dot	/d/	_____
map	/m/	_____
sad	/s/	_____
talk	/t/	_____
cow	/k/	_____
bird	/b/	_____

Score _____/6

Task 3: Sound Blending

Task: The child will listen to word sounds and will blend the sounds together to say the word.

Model: I am going to say some sounds. Then I want you to put the sounds together to make a word. I will do the first one. Listen to the sounds: /r/-/u/-/n/. When I put the sounds /r/-/u/-/n/ together, they make the word *run*.

Sample: Listen to these sounds: /k/-/a/-/t/. What word do you make when you put /k/-/a/-/t/ together? (cat) You're correct. /k/-/a/-/t/ makes the word *cat*. Now listen again. I will say some sounds. You put the sounds together to make a word and tell me the word.

Child's name _____

Date _____

	Correct Response	Child's Response
/g/-/ō/	go	_____
/sh/-/ē/-/p/	sheep	_____
/j/-/u/-/m/-/p/	jump	_____
/a/-/n/-/t/	ant	_____
/h/-/o/-/t/	hot	_____
/l/-/i/-/p/	lip	_____
/d/-/e/-/s/-/k/	desk	_____
/b/-/ī/	by	_____

Score _____/8

Task 4: Sound Segmenting

Task: The child will listen to a word and then will produce each phoneme in the word separately.

Model: I am going to say a word. Then I am going to say each sound in the word. Listen carefully for each sound. The word is *go*. The sounds in *go* are /g/-/ō/. (Be sure to articulate each sound separately. Do not simply stretch out the word.)

Sample: Listen to this word. This time you tell me the sounds in the word. Listen carefully: *man*. What sounds do you hear in *man*? (/m/-/a/-/n/) You are correct. The sounds in the word *man* are /m/-/a/-/n/.

Now listen to some more words. Tell me the sounds you hear in these words.

Child's name _____

Date _____

	Correct Response	Child's Response
dog	/d/-/ô/-/g/	_____
keep	/k/-/ē/-/p/	_____
no	/n/-/ō/	_____
that	/th/-/a/-/t/	_____
me	/m/-/ē/	_____
do	/d/-/oō/	_____
race	/r/-/ā/-/s/	_____
in	/i/-/n/	_____

Score _____/8

Summary of Performance Form
Phonemic Awareness Interview

Child's Name_____ Grade_____ Date_____

Understanding of Concept

0–10 = Minimal   **11–20** = Limited   **21–30** = Good

Child's Score:

Sound Matching _____/8 Comments:_____
_____
_____

Sound Isolation _____/6 Comments:_____
_____
_____

Sound Blending _____/8 Comments:_____
_____
_____

Sound Segmenting _____/8 Comments:_____
_____
_____

Total _____/ 30 **Understanding of Phonemic Awareness**_____

Comments: _____
_____
_____

Inventory of Concepts About Print

Materials: Select a short storybook with pictures at the top of the page and several lines of text at the bottom. The child may point with a pencil.

Directions: Turn to the title page and read aloud the following information from the book:

> **Title of Book**
> **Author's Name**
> **Illustrator's Name**

Turn to the first page of the story and read all of the questions below to the child.

Task 1 Book and Print Awareness Task	Middle of Year Score (0 or 1)	End of Year Score (0 or 1)
1. If I am going to read this story, where do I begin to read? Point to where I start reading. (Correct: Child must point to the first word of the first paragraph.)	_____	_____
2. Show me a sentence. Point to where it starts and ends. (Correct: Child must point to the beginning and end of a sentence on the page.)	_____	_____
3. Show me a word. (Correct: Child must point to a word on the page.)	_____	_____
4. Show me a letter. (Correct: Child must point to a letter in a word.)	_____	_____
5. Show me a capital letter. (Correct: Child must point to a capital letter.)	_____	_____
Total Correct: (5 total)	_____	_____

Inventory of Emergent Reading

Directions: Place in front of the child three books that are familiar to him or her. Choose books with a story line rather than ABC or other basic-concept books. Ask the child to select one of the books. Explain that he or she is to start at the beginning and read it to you as well as he or she can. Using the chart below, enter today's date next to the stage of emergent reading that best describes the child's rendering of the story. The same chart may be reused for additional assessments.

Name _____ Teacher _____

	Date	Date	Date
Picture-governed, story not formed (Child reads by labeling and commenting on pictures. Little or no evidence of connected story line.)			
Picture-governed, oral language used (Child focuses on pictures and uses an oral language style in narration. May tell an interesting story, but language is unlike that of book.)			
Picture-governed, more written language used (Child alternates between oral language style and "reading intonation" and wording that sounds like written language. At times, rendering might sound very much like written language of book.)			
Print-governed (Child reads text in conventional manner.)			

Comments: _____

_____

_____

_____

Name _____

Capital/Lowercase Letter Inventory

Sample ☆ F	t ○	B ○	f ●
1. z	N ○	w ○	Z ○
2. a	A ○	n ○	B ○
3. Y	y ○	T ○	c ○
4. b	D ○	B ○	f ○
5. X	C ○	x ○	Q ○

GO ON ▶

42 Assessment: Emergent Literacy in Kindergarten

Name _____

Capital/Lowercase Letter Inventory

6. c	C ○	Z ○	t ○
7. W	s ○	w ○	N ○
8. d	F ○	b ○	D ○
9. V	W ○	r ○	v ○
10. e	g ○	E ○	a ○
11. U	L ○	I ○	u ○

GO ON

Name _____

Capital/Lowercase Letter Inventory

12. f	F ○	y ○	B ○
13. T	k ○	t ○	M ○
14. g	o ○	G ○	j ○
15. S	q ○	A ○	s ○
16. h	Y ○	i ○	H ○
17. R	r ○	P ○	e ○

GO ON

Name _____

Capital/Lowercase Letter Inventory

18.	i	R ○	V ○	I ○
19.	Q	q ○	K ○	f ○
20.	j	J ○	Z ○	b ○
21.	P	d ○	S ○	p ○
22.	k	g ○	K ○	T ○
23.	O	M ○	o ○	a ○

GO ON

Name _____

Capital/Lowercase Letter Inventory

24. I	L ○	v ○	t ○
25. N	X ○	j ○	n ○
26. m	s ○	M ○	l ○
27. Z	z ○	D ○	C ○
28. A	h ○	L ○	a ○
29. y	Y ○	z ○	c ○

GO ON

Name _____

Capital/Lowercase Letter Inventory

30.	B	I ○	P ○	b ○
31.	x	g ○	X ○	p ○
32.	C	c ○	H ○	F ○
33.	w	q ○	W ○	v ○
34.	D	J ○	d ○	a ○
35.	v	i ○	h ○	V ○

GO ON

Name _____

Capital/Lowercase Letter Inventory

36. E	e ○ S ○ K ○
37. u	N ○ d ○ U ○
38. F	f ○ w ○ X ○
39. t	l ○ T ○ q ○
40. G	K ○ n ○ g ○
41. s	S ○ c ○ D ○

GO ON

48 Assessment: Emergent Literacy in Kindergarten

Name _____

Capital/Lowercase Letter Inventory

42. H	Q ○	h ○	y ○
43. r	R ○	G ○	m ○
44. I	O ○	i ○	b ○
45. q	r ○	E ○	Q ○
46. J	V ○	j ○	z ○
47. p	g ○	f ○	P ○

GO ON

Emergent Literacy Inventories 49

Name _____

Capital/Lowercase Letter Inventory

48. K	R ○	b ○	k ○
49. o	e ○	O ○	d ○
50. L	l ○	F ○	c ○
51. M	m ○	D ○	Z ○
52. n	N ○	x ○	A ○

STOP

Name _____

PART A: Matching Beginning Sounds Inventory

Sample

1.

2.

3.

4.

GO ON

Emergent Literacy Inventories 51

Name _____

PART A: Matching Beginning Sounds Inventory

5.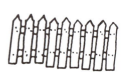

6.

7.

8.

GO ON ▶

52 Assessment: Emergent Literacy in Kindergarten

Name _____

PART A: Matching Beginning Sounds Inventory

9. 	
10. 	  
11. 	
12. 	

GO ON ➤

Emergent Literacy Inventories 53

Name _____

PART A: Matching Beginning Sounds Inventory

13. 	
14. 	
15. 	
16. 	 

GO ON ▶

54 Assessment: Emergent Literacy in Kindergarten

Name _____

PART A: Matching Beginning Sounds Inventory

17. 	
18. 	
19. 	 
20. 	 

STOP

Emergent Literacy Inventories 55

Name _____

PART B: Matching Beginning Sounds Inventory

Sample

21.

22.

23.

24.

GO ON

56 Assessment: Emergent Literacy in Kindergarten

Name _____

PART B: Matching Beginning Sounds Inventory

25. 	
26. 	
27. 	
28. 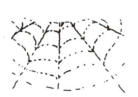	

GO ON

Name _____

PART B: Matching Beginning Sounds Inventory

29.

30.

31.

32.

GO ON

58 Assessment: Emergent Literacy in Kindergarten

Name _____

PART B: Matching Beginning Sounds Inventory

33.

34.

35.

36.

GO ON

Emergent Literacy Inventories 59

Name _____

PART B: Matching Beginning Sounds Inventory

37.

38.

39.

40.

GO ON

60 Assessment: Emergent Literacy in Kindergarten

Name _____

PART B: Matching Beginning Sounds Inventory

41.

42.

43.

44.

GO ON

Emergent Literacy Inventories 61

Name _____

PART B: Matching Beginning Sounds Inventory

45.

46.

47.

48.

62 Assessment: Emergent Literacy in Kindergarten

Name _____

PART A: Matching Letters and Beginning Sounds Inventory

Sample ★ p	
1. m	
2. s	
3. j	
4. t	

GO ON

Emergent Literacy Inventories 63

Name _____

PART A: Matching Letters and Beginning Sounds Inventory

5. c	sock ○	cup ○	ball ○
6. f	fence ○	cat ○	donkey ○
7. d	mouse ○	balloon ○	dog ○
8. a	sandwich ○	alligator ○	bell ○

GO ON ▶

64 Assessment: Emergent Literacy in Kindergarten

Name _____

PART A: Matching Letters and Beginning Sounds Inventory

9. h — jar ○   box ○   hose ○

10. b — pencil ○   bib ○   duck ○

11. m — bird ○   fish ○   mouse ○

12. c — car ○   sun ○   doll ○

GO ON

Emergent Literacy Inventories 65

Name _____

PART A: Matching Letters and Beginning Sounds Inventory

13. t	
14. f	
15. p	
16. d	

GO ON

Name _____

PART A: Matching Letters and Beginning Sounds Inventory

17. s	
18. e	
19. j	
20. h	

GO ON

Emergent Literacy Inventories 67

Name _____

PART A: Matching Letters and Beginning Sounds Inventory

21. t	
22. a	
23. s	
24. e	

STOP

Name _____

PART B: Matching Letters and Beginning Sounds Inventory

Sample ☆ W	(leaf) ○ (wagon) ● (dog) ○
25. r	(jacks) ○ (vest) ○ (ring) ○
26. o	(helicopter) ○ (cucumber) ○ (ostrich) ○
27. k	(nest) ○ (king) ○ (toothbrush) ○
28. l	(leaf) ○ (bell) ○ (fish) ○

GO ON

Name _____

PART B: Matching Letters and Beginning Sounds Inventory

29. i

30. c

31. w

32. t

GO ON

70 Assessment: Emergent Literacy in Kindergarten

Name _____

PART B: Matching Letters and Beginning Sounds Inventory

33. v	(fence) ○ (vest) ○ (mole) ○
34. p	(doll) ○ (yo-yo) ○ (balloon) ○
35. n	(house) ○ (nest) ○ (goose) ○
36. u	(tree) ○ (car) ○ (umbrella) ○

GO ON

Emergent Literacy Inventories 71

Name _____

PART B: Matching Letters and Beginning Sounds Inventory

37. y	
38. f	
39. a	
40. d	

GO ON

72 Assessment: Emergent Literacy in Kindergarten

Name _____

PART B: Matching Letters and Beginning Sounds Inventory

41. z	(fox) (zebra) (pig) ○ ○ ○
42. h	(yo-yo) (wagon) (house) ○ ○ ○
43. r	(mouse) (rake) (leaf) ○ ○ ○
44. j	(cucumber) (king) (jar) ○ ○ ○

GO ON

Name _____

PART B: Matching Letters and Beginning Sounds Inventory

45. e	
46. s	
47. g	
48. u	

STOP

74 Assessment: Emergent Literacy in Kindergarten

Answer Key

Capital/Lowercase Letter Inventory

1. Z
2. A
3. y
4. B
5. x
6. C
7. w
8. D
9. v
10. E
11. u
12. F
13. t
14. G
15. s
16. H
17. r
18. I
19. q
20. J
21. p
22. K
23. o
24. L
25. n
26. M
27. z
28. a
29. Y
30. b
31. X
32. c
33. W
34. d
35. V
36. e
37. U
38. f
39. T
40. g
41. S
42. h
43. R
44. i
45. Q
46. j
47. P
48. k
49. O
50. l
51. m
52. N

Matching Beginning Sounds Inventory

Part A
1. bell
2. moon
3. cup
4. pie
5. fox
6. sock
7. apple
8. book
9. toothbrush
10. mouse
11. pencil
12. astronaut
13. seal
14. helicopter
15. tiger
16. car
17. dog
18. sun
19. mop
20. elf

Part B
21. necklace
22. pan
23. nail
24. elephant
25. soap
26. table
27. vest
28. watch
29. rake
30. olive
31. lion
32. igloo
33. yo-yo
34. zebra
35. ball
36. cage
37. deer
38. fork
39. octopus
40. heart
41. jet
42. keys
43. lock
44. moon
45. ostrich
46. web
47. up
48. nail

Answer Key

Matching Letters and Beginning Sounds Inventory

Part A

1. mitten
2. seal
3. jar
4. tent
5. cup
6. fence
7. dog
8. alligator
9. hose
10. bib
11. mouse
12. car
13. toothbrush
14. fox
15. pickle
16. duck
17. sock
18. envelope
19. jacks
20. hammer
21. toothbrush
22. ax
23. seal
24. elf

Matching Letters and Beginning Sounds Inventory

Part B

25. ring
26. ostrich
27. king
28. leaf
29. igloo
30. can
31. wagon
32. table
33. vest
34. puppet
35. nest
36. umbrella
37. yo-yo
38. fish
39. ax
40. doll
41. zebra
42. house
43. rake
44. jar
45. elephant
46. sandwich
47. goat
48. up

Theme Tests

Using the Theme Tests

Tests 1–12

"Treat an assessment session as you would any other class activity."

Using the Theme Tests

These tests are designed to assess children's understanding of the letters and sounds presented in each theme. Adapt the following samples to administer each test.

Sample for Task 1 (Theme Test 1 page 79):
Point to the letter in the first box and tell me its name. (*m*) **Now point to the three letters next to *m*. Which one is exactly the same? Fill in the circle under the letter.** (You may also wish to have the child indicate which letter is the capital or lowercase form of the first letter.)

Sample for Task 2 (Theme Test 1 page 79):
Name the picture in the first box. (monkey) Tell me the sound you hear at the beginning of *monkey*. (/m/) Now say the names of the pictures in that row. Fill in the circles under the pictures that begin with the same sound. (See Response Key below.)

Response Key for the Theme Tests
Picture names are listed below for each item in Task 2. Answers are in boldface.

Theme 1, page 79
monkey, **mouse**, fox, **moon**
fish, mop, **foot**, **fork**

Theme 2, page 80
ball, moon, **bat**, **bear**
seal, **sandwich**, fish, saw

Theme 3, page 81
jacks, **jar**, bee, **jet**
pig, **pencil**, **pan**, mitten

Theme 4, page 82
hat, **horse**, **hammer**, bus
duck, sock, **dog**, **desk**

Theme 5, page 83
carrots, **car**, deer, **cat**
alligator, **apple**, **ants**, sun

Theme 6, page 84
tiger, **ten**, **turtle**, pillow
elephant, house, **eggs**, **envelope**

Theme 7, page 85
yarn, **yo-yo**, bus, **yak**
zebra, octopus, **zipper**, **zero**

Theme 8, page 86
kite, **keys**, igloo, **kangaroo**
window, **watermelon**, **wagon**, iguana

Theme 9, page 87
ladder, **lamp**, umbrella, **lion**
vest, up, **violin**, **van**

Theme 10, page 88
nest, **needle**, goat, **nut**
rabbit, seal, **ring**, **rake**

Theme 11, page 89
Note: Pictures in the first row *end* in /x/.
box, **six**, **fox**, bird
question mark, **queen**, table, **quilt**

Theme 12, page 90
Children should draw a line between each group of words and the picture it describes.

78 Assessment: Emergent Literacy in Kindergarten

Theme 1 Test

Child's Name_____ Date_____

m	M ○	F ○	m ○
F	F ○	f ○	M ○

Theme 1 Test 79

Theme 2 Test

Child's Name_____ Date_____

B	b ○	S ○	B ○
s	S ○	s ○	b ○

80 Theme 2 Test

Theme 3 Test

Child's Name_____ Date_____

j	J ◯	p ◯	j ◯
P	p ◯	P ◯	J ◯

Theme 4 Test

Child's Name_____ Date_____

h	d ○	h ○	H ○
D	H ○	d ○	D ○

82 Theme 4 Test

Theme 5 Test

Child's Name_____ Date_____

C	a ○	C ○	c ○
a	a ○	c ○	A ○

Harcourt

Theme 5 Test

Theme 6 Test

Child's Name_____ Date_____

t	E ○	T ○	t ○
E	e ○	E ○	T ○

84 Theme 6 Test

Theme 7 Test

Child's Name_____ Date_____

Y	Y ○	y ○	z ○
O	o ○	Y ○	O ○
z	Z ○	z ○	O ○

Theme 7 Test 85

Theme 8 Test

Child's Name_____ Date_____

k	K ○	i ○	k ○
I	i ○	I ○	w ○
w	W ○	w ○	k ○

Theme 9 Test

Child's Name_____ Date_____

U	u ○	V ○	U ○
L	L ○	I ○	U ○
v	u ○	v ○	V ○

Theme 10 Test

Child's Name_____ Date_____

n	N ○	g ○	n ○
G	R ○	G ○	g ○
r	r ○	n ○	R ○

88 Theme 10 Test

Theme 11 Test

Child's Name_____ Date_____

Theme 12 Test (Review)

Child's Name_____ Date_____

the cat in a hat

a cap on a map

A dad is sad.

a ram and a ham

Performance Assessment

Introduction to Performance Assessment

Story:
That Bothered Kate
Response activity, model papers

Story:
Nellie's Knot
Response activity, model papers

Story:
My Friend Whale
Response activity, model papers

"The performance assessment should be used just like any other classroom shared reading activity."

Introduction to Performance Assessment

The performance assessments are designed as benchmarks to help a teacher gauge each child's language development.

Like the emergent literacy inventories, these structured activities should not be seen as being more important than the ongoing observations you make while kid watching, conferencing with children about their portfolios, and so on. However, the activities do provide another opportunity to assess children's progress.

What are the benchmark assessments and when are they used?

Each of the three benchmark assessments consists of a story for shared reading, followed by a suggested written response. The first one can be used early in the school year after children are comfortable with the classroom routine. Use the second assessment early in the second half of the year, and the third near the end of the year.

How are the performance assessments administered?

By working with a group of six or seven children at a time, you can maximize your chances to observe what each of them can do. You can also help any children who may be anxious or uncertain about the task.

The performance assessment should be used just like any other shared reading activity:

1. Beforehand, build background and help children make predictions about story characters and events.

2. Do a shared reading with the children, pausing to let them discuss pictures and make predictions.

3. After reading, encourage several children to tell their reactions to the story. During the discussion, try to gauge children's level of participation. Are they contributing ideas? Do they seem to have a sense of story sequence? Can they interpret characters' feelings?

4. During the written response, encourage children to write about the pictures they are drawing. As children finish, have them tell you about their pictures, and ask them if you can write their ideas on the back. These comments will help you later as you evaluate their responses.

THAT BOTHERED KATE

by Sally Noll

Kate's little sister, Tory,
was a copycat.
And that bothered Kate.

Everything Kate did,
Tory wanted to do, too.
Everything.

"It's part of growing up," her mother would assure her. "She needs you."

But there just wasn't anything Kate did that Tory didn't want to try.

She wanted to look like Kate.

Once their neighbor Mrs. Potts said, "My, you look just like twins," even though she knew they weren't.

And that bothered Kate.

101

Double peppermint chocolate chip was Kate's favorite ice cream.

It was Tory's favorite, too.

And that bothered Kate the most.

Then one day Alex asked Tory to ride with him.

The next week Annie from across the street invited Tory to play.

After that Tory and
Annie played often...

and sometimes Tory just wanted to play alone.

It seemed to Kate that
Tory hardly noticed her.
And that bothered Kate.

"Is this part of growing up, too?" Kate asked.

"Yes," said her mother. "I am afraid this is part of growing up, too."

"But she doesn't need me anymore," said Kate sadly.

"Oh, yes, she does," said her mother.

"In so many ways. And right now she needs you to hold her hand crossing the street while you both go to the ice cream store."

As they went down the street, Kate asked, "Tory, what flavor are you going to have?"

"Double peppermint chocolate chip, of course," said Tory.

And that didn't bother Kate at all.

Children's Responses

That Bothered Kate
by Sally Noll

Suggested Response Activity:
Draw a picture of what bothered Kate.

Following are three model responses to the writing task above. Their scores range from a "3" to a "1." A score of 3 can be thought of as an indicator of "excellent" comprehension; a score of 2 can be thought of as an indicator of "adequate" comprehension; and a score of 1 as an indicator of "minimal" comprehension. Use these papers as anchor points as you weigh and balance different aspects of each child's response.

Score 3

This child's picture and writing reveal an excellent response to the question "Draw a picture of what bothered Kate." When asked to read what was written, the child said, "Katy's sister copied her dressing up." The child had clearly drawn and written about something from the story that bothered Kate. The drawing shows that the child understands the main idea of the story. The writing reveals that the student knows the difference between letters and words, has knowledge of left-to-right sequence, and is able to represent sounds (phonemes) with appropriate letters (graphemes). The child has both encoded (written) ideas and has decoded what was written by reading aloud what was written. The emergent literacy skills of this child rate a score of 3.

Score 2

This child's picture and writing reveal an adequate response to the question "Draw a picture of what bothered Kate." When asked to read what was written, the child said, "Katie sister ate the same ice cream." The student has drawn and told about one of the incidents that bothered Kate. It is clear that the student understood that what bothered Kate was that her sister copied what she did. The student has grasped the main idea of the story. However, the response is not as well developed as the model 3 paper. The writing is less mature. The student may have an emerging understanding of the difference between letters and words. There is some relationship between sounds (phonemes) and letters (graphemes). For example, the "KT" at the top of the paper and the "the" at the bottom right indicate developing writing skills. The student was able to say what she had written and has a concept of writing and reading what was written. This student is typical of many kindergarten children who are developing as beginning readers and writers. This response represents a model 2 paper at this level.

Score 1

This child's picture and writing reveal a limited response to the question "Draw a picture of what bothered Kate." When asked to read what was written, the child said, "Kate rode a scooter." The response is not an answer to the question, and it is difficult to tell if the picture matches what the child said was written. The child may have felt that Kate wanted to ride by herself, but there is no representation of that understanding in either the picture or what the child said was written. The writing reveals that the child has only a very basic knowledge that letters are used to represent meaning. However, there seems to be no knowledge of the difference between letters and words nor any knowledge of the relationship between sounds (phonemes) and letters (graphemes). The emergent literacy skills of this child rate a score of 1.

Nellie had tied a knot in her trunk to remind herself of something very special. But now she had forgotten what it was! She tried and tried, but she just couldn't remember. "I'm not going to untie this knot until I do remember," thought Nellie.

But a knot in your trunk gives you all sorts of problems.

"Keep up, Nellie. Keep in line!"

But Nellie couldn't keep in line.

"Don't forget to wash behind your ears, Nellie!"

But Nellie couldn't wash behind her ears.

"Eat your breakfast, Nellie!"
But Nellie couldn't eat her breakfast.

"Catch the bananas, Nellie!"
But Nellie couldn't catch the bananas.

"Blow up the balloons, Nellie!"

But Nellie couldn't blow up the balloons.

"Help us put the streamers up, Nellie!"

But Nellie couldn't. She got into a terrible tangle.

Poor Nellie, she couldn't do anything right, and she still couldn't remember why she had tied a knot in her trunk.

"Come and stir the cake, Nellie, and don't forget to wish!" But, although Nellie couldn't stir the cake, she

could wish. "I wish . . . I wish . . . I wish I knew why I tied a knot in my trunk!"

But still Nellie couldn't remember.

She went off by herself to have a good, long think. Then . . . as she was wandering sadly through the

jungle, not noticing where she was going, she stumbled into a clearing. All the animals seemed to be having a party.

"Come on, Nellie! Blow out the candle!"

Nellie took a deep breath and blew as hard as she could.

She blew so hard that out went the candle . . . and Nellie's knot!

"HAPPY BIRTHDAY, NELLIE!"

Suddenly, Nellie knew why she had tied a knot in her trunk—to remember her birthday!

Children's Responses

Nellie's Knot
by Ken Brown

Suggested Response Activity:
Draw a picture of one of the things Nellie couldn't do.

Following are three model responses to the writing task above. Their scores range from a "3" to a "1." A score of 3 can be thought of as an indicator of "excellent" comprehension; a score of 2 can be thought of as an indicator of "adequate" comprehension; and a score of 1 as an indicator of "minimal" comprehension. Use these papers as anchor points as you weigh and balance different aspects of each child's response.

Score 3

This child's picture and writing reveal a well-developed response to the prompt *Draw a picture of one of the things Nellie couldn't do*. When asked to read what was written, the child said, "Nellie couldn't blow the candles." She has clearly drawn and written about something from the story even though it is something Nellie could do. The picture shows Nellie and the candles. The writing reveals that the child has some knowledge of the difference between letters and words and of left-to-right sequence. She expresses her ideas with letters to represent some sounds. The emergent literacy skills of this child rate a score of 3.

Score 2

This child's picture and writing are an adequate response to the prompt *Draw a picture of one of the things Nellie couldn't do*. When asked to read what was written, the child said, "She can't catch a banana." The picture clearly demonstrates that incident from the story. However, the writing is not as advanced as that of the model 3 paper. It is not clear whether the child recognizes the difference between letters and words. There is some relationship between the letters that are written and what the child read, but the writing does not reveal a well-developed knowledge of the relationship between letters and sounds. The emergent literacy skills of this child rate a score of 2.

Score 1

This child's picture and writing demonstrate a limited response to the prompt. When asked to read what was written, she said, "Nellie cannot blow the balloons." The picture is not a good representation of that story event. The writing is limited and does not reveal knowledge of the relationship between letters and sounds. The child's ability to tell about a story event, draw a picture, and add some letters indicates that she is beginning to develop literacy skills. The emergent literacy skills of this child rate a score of 1.

MY FRIEND WHALE

by Simon James

My friend Whale and I swim together every night.

My friend Whale is a blue whale.

My friend Whale makes the biggest splash of any sea creature, but he is a very slow and graceful swimmer.

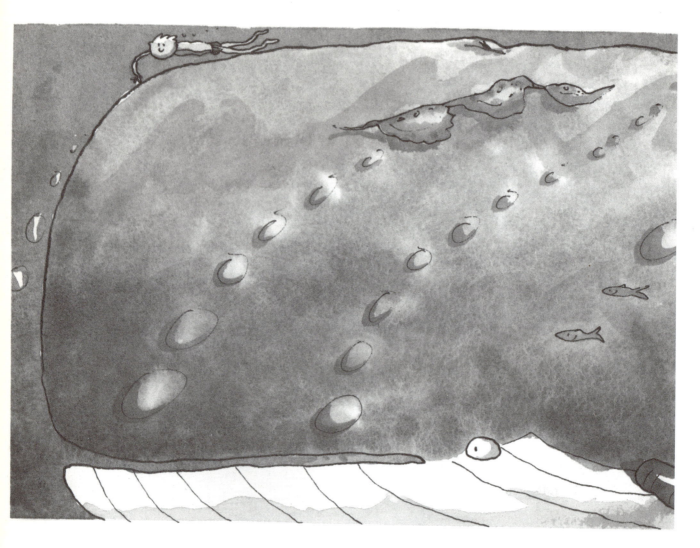

My friend Whale is the biggest and heaviest animal on land or in the sea.

You may think, because he is so large, that he must be dangerous.

But my friend Whale has no teeth.

In fact, he only eats fishy things smaller than my little finger.

My friend Whale can hold his breath underwater for almost an hour.

But because he is not a fish, he has to come up for air just like me.

My friend Whale can't smell anything.

My friend Whale can't taste anything.

But he has very good ears—he can hear an underwater world of things that I can't.

My friend Whale speaks with squeaking, clicking, and whistling sounds.

Other whales can hear him from a hundred miles away.

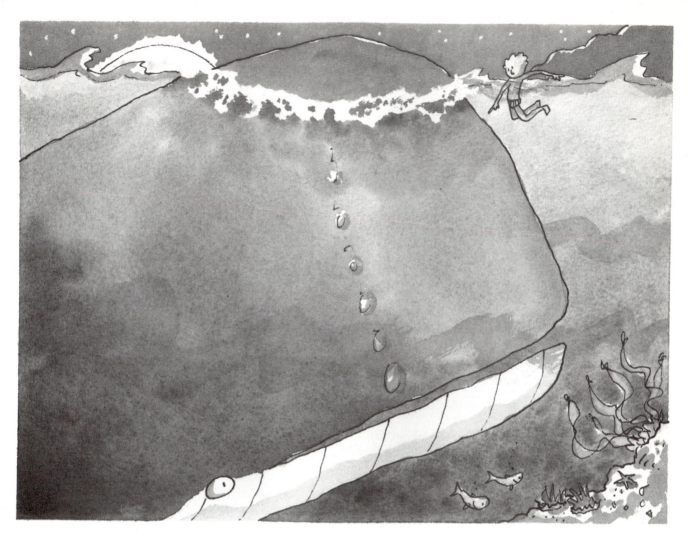

My friend Whale has very sensitive skin. He can feel the slightest touch.

That is the way I say good-bye for the night. See you tomorrow, my friend Whale.

My friend Whale really does make the biggest splash. But the next night, I don't see the spray of his spout or the splash of his tail.

He didn't come for me at all.

My friend Whale didn't come last night either, or the night before. Maybe he's found a new friend.

Or maybe something has happened to him. Now my friend Whale only visits in my dreams.

Children's Responses

My Friend Whale
by Simon James

Suggested Response Activity:

Have children draw and write some new things they learned about whales that they want to tell a friend.

Following are three model responses to the writing task above. Their scores range from a "3" to a "1." A score of 3 can be thought of as an indicator of "excellent" comprehension; a score of 2 can be thought of as an indicator of "adequate" comprehension; and a score of 1 as an indicator of "minimal" comprehension. Use these papers as anchor points as you weigh and balance different aspects of each child's response.

Score 3

This child's picture and writing demonstrate an excellent understanding of the text and the task to write to her friend something new she learned about whales. The picture clearly shows the whale and the boy "riding" on it. The child writes that whales are graceful and they eat tiny fish. The command of letters and words is excellent. The emergent literacy skills of this child rate a score of 3.

Teacher's Edition / Grade K

Score 2

The child demonstrates that he understood the task and the facts in the story. While not as sophisticated as the 3 model, the child does draw a picture of a whale. When the teacher asked what he had written about the whale, the child responded that he wrote "Whales can hear very well." It is not difficult to pick out the beginning development of sound/symbol relationships. However, this child has not yet developed a sense of the separation of groups of letters into words. The writing is at an adequate level for a child at this age.

150 Assessment: Emergent Literacy in Kindergarten

Score 1

This child's drawing is not very comprehensible. When asked about the picture, the child said that he had drawn a whale and a cobra and said that the picture was about the story. It seems that the child did not comprehend the task, and it is difficult to determine why he drew the cobra except that he may have been thinking about other animals. The child did not attempt any writing to explain the picture. The response is at a minimal level.

151